LENNY
AND THE VERY BIG SHOW

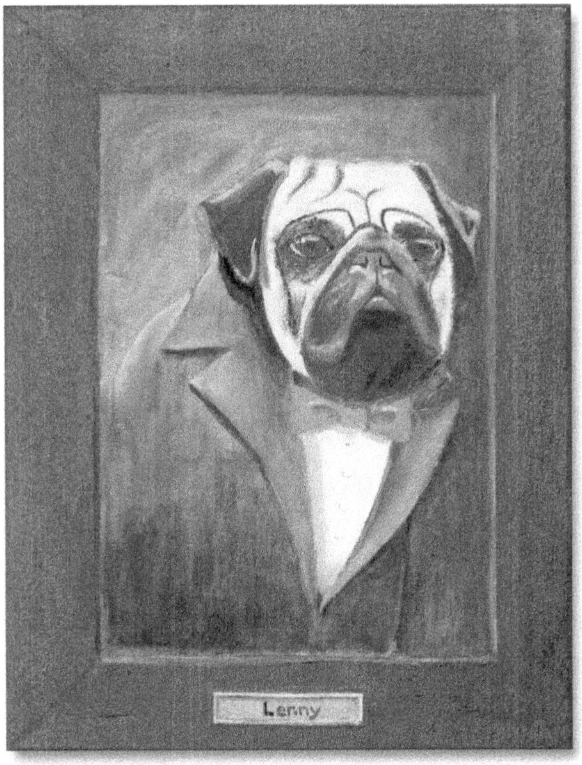
Lenny

TEXT AND ILLUSTRATIONS BY

P.V. LARSSEN

To my family.

Lenny of the golden tower
Had the money, wanted power,
So he channeled P.T. Barnum
Just to see if he could charm 'em.

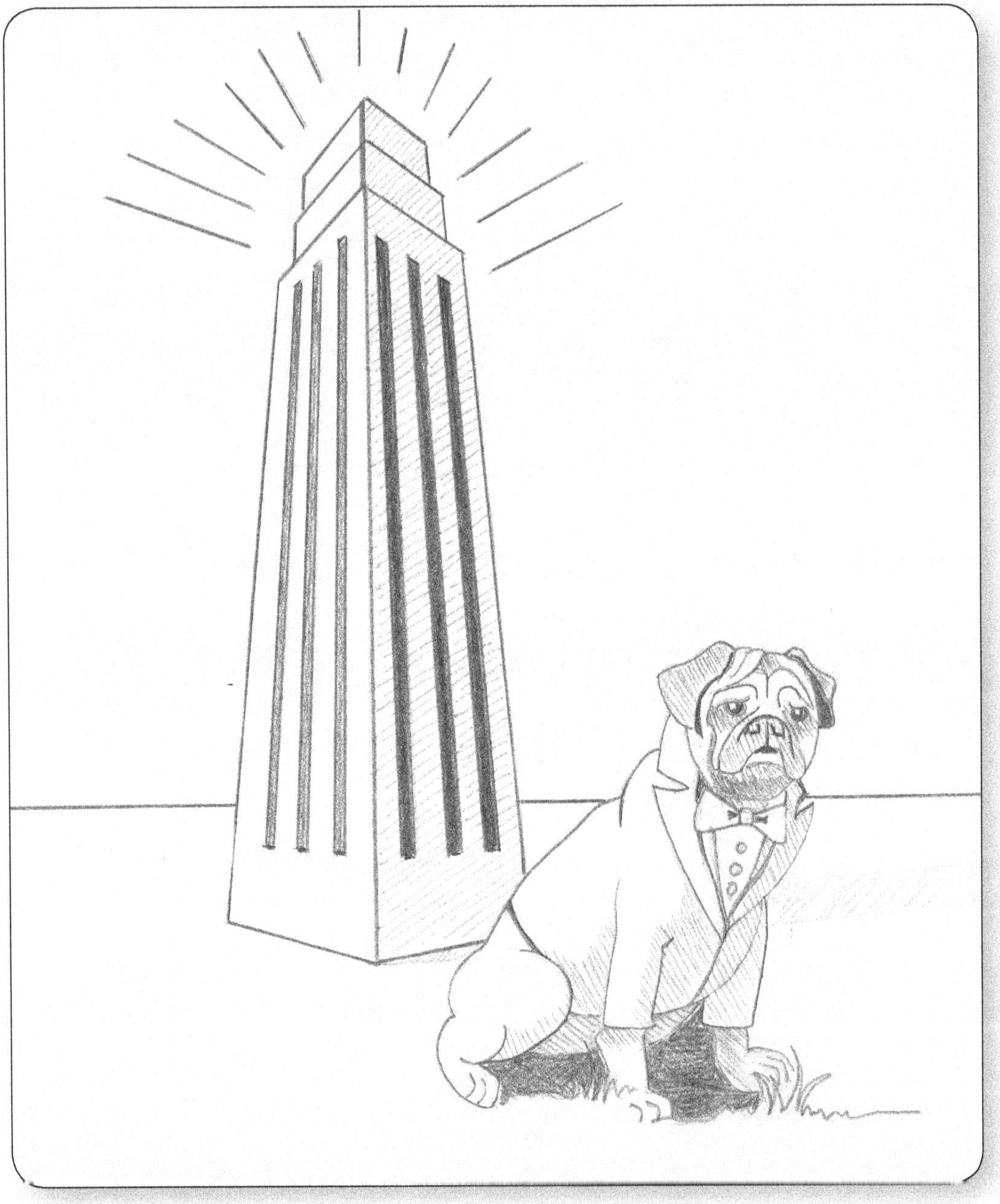

So like fish to bait are drawn,
Lenny's audience trailed along
To view the wonders of his show
And to see how far he'd go.

Others tried to face him down

But it was hard to best a clown.

He made crowds laugh, he made them roar,

And then he showed his foes the door.

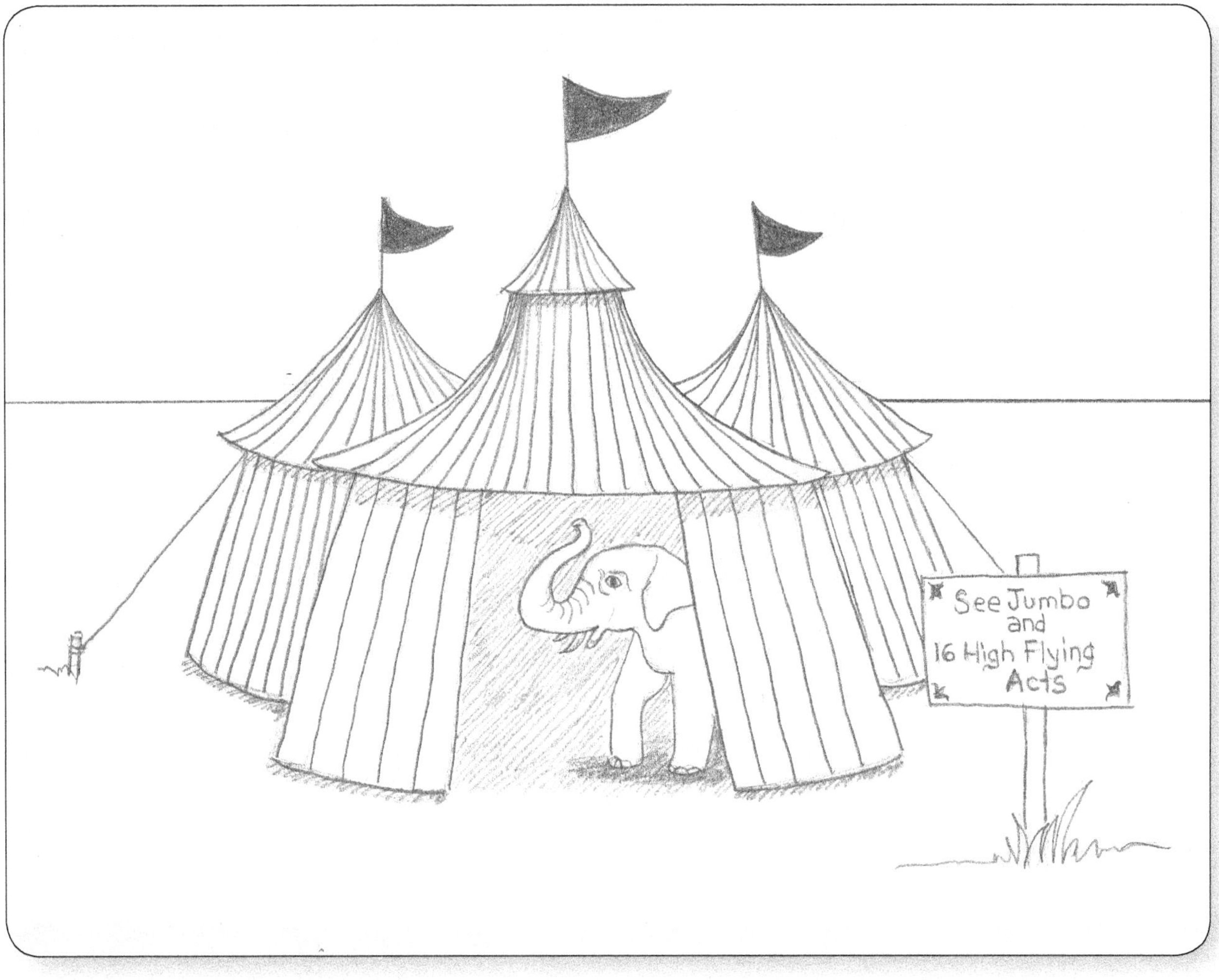
See Jumbo
and
16 High Flying
Acts

Now the bankers couldn't wait
 To get part of the power and the gate.
 They threw their money on the floor,
"Use our acts; we'll give you more."

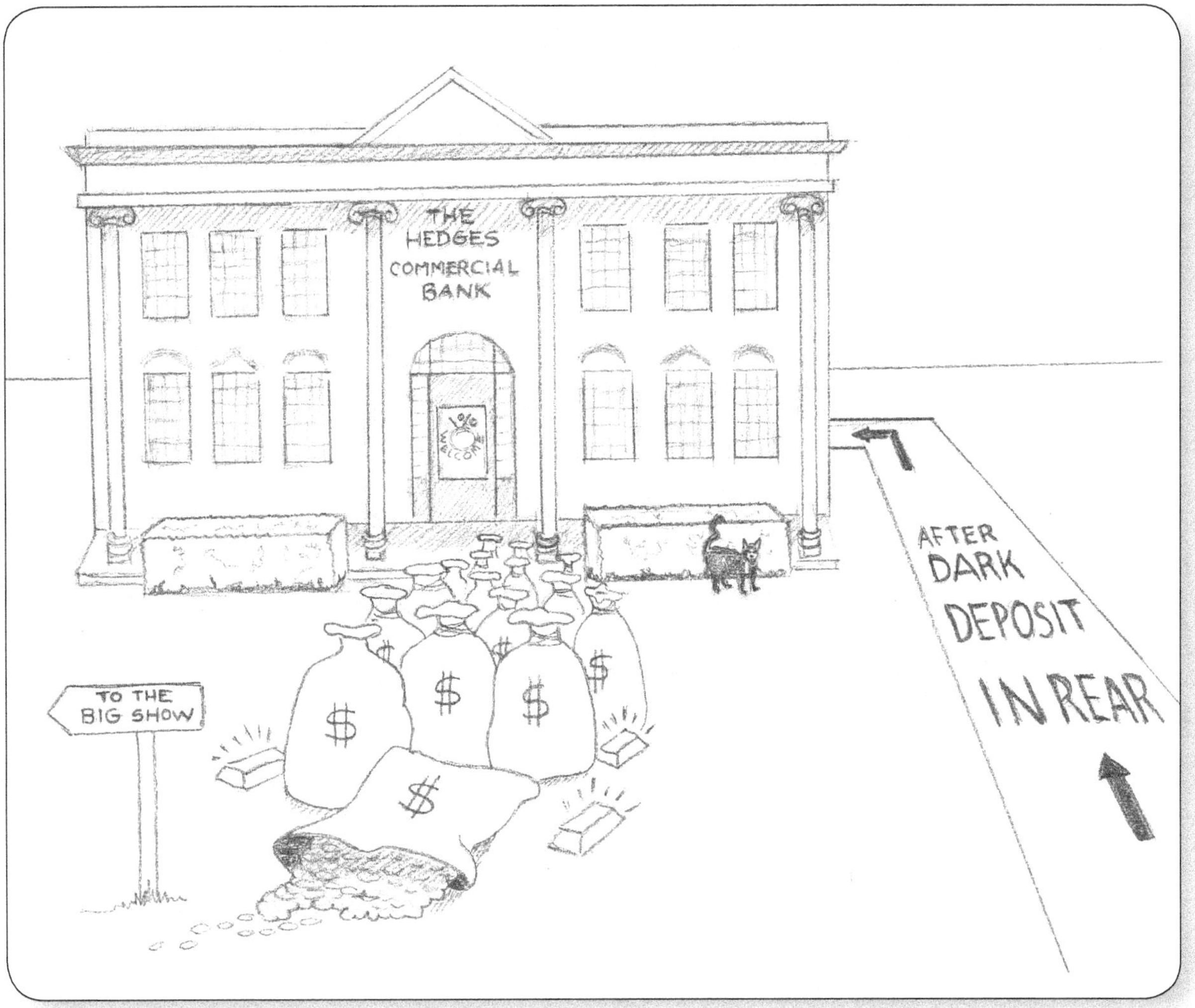
THE HEDGES COMMERCIAL BANK
1%
WELCOME
AFTER DARK DEPOSIT IN REAR
TO THE BIG SHOW

So he hired the Sphinx to guard the gate,

To riddle the press and make them wait.

He also brought the walrus along

To feed bay oysters to the throng.

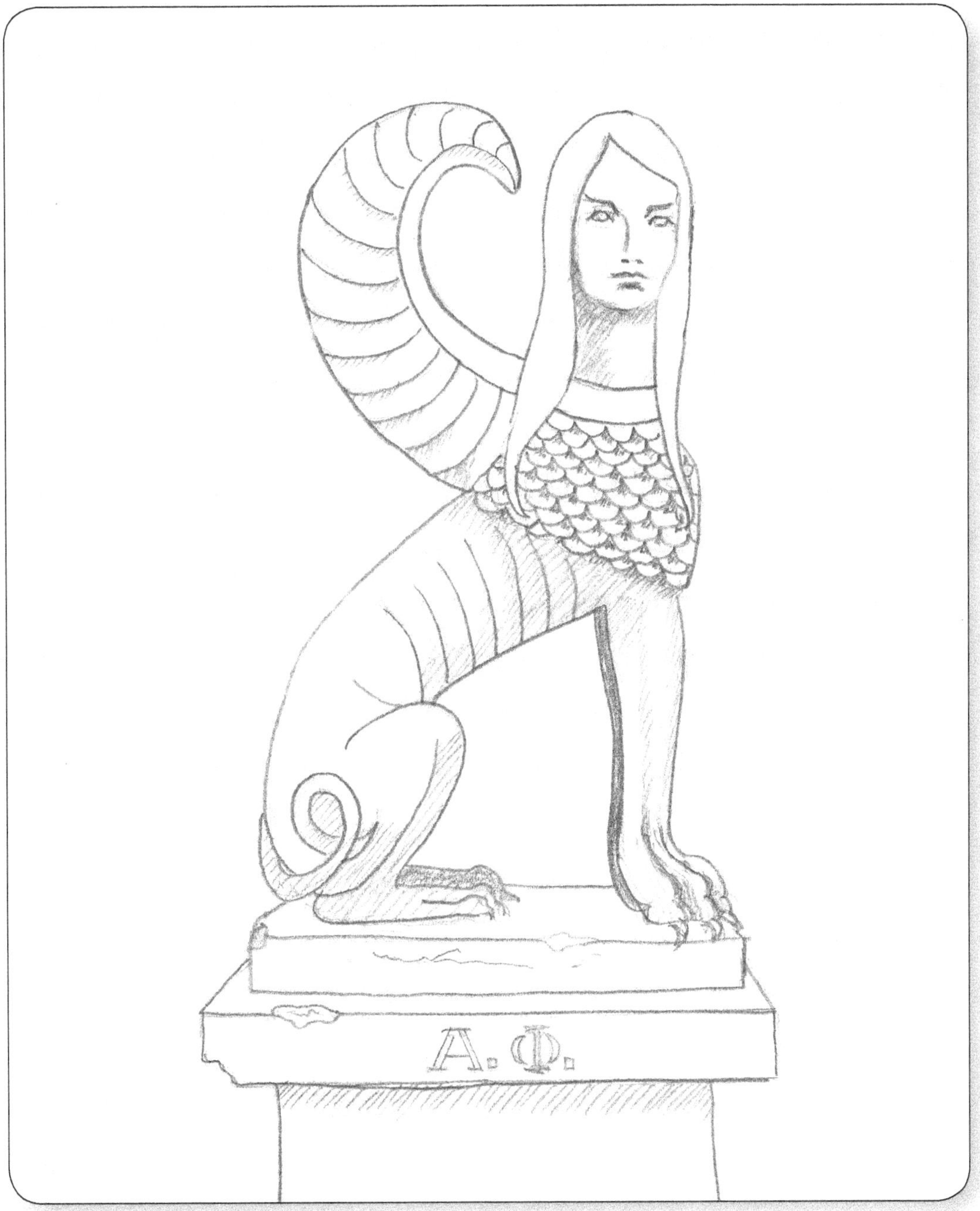
Α. Φ.

Then Lenny brought his cast and crew
To the show to determine who
Through votes would win the golden ring
And be anointed queen or king.

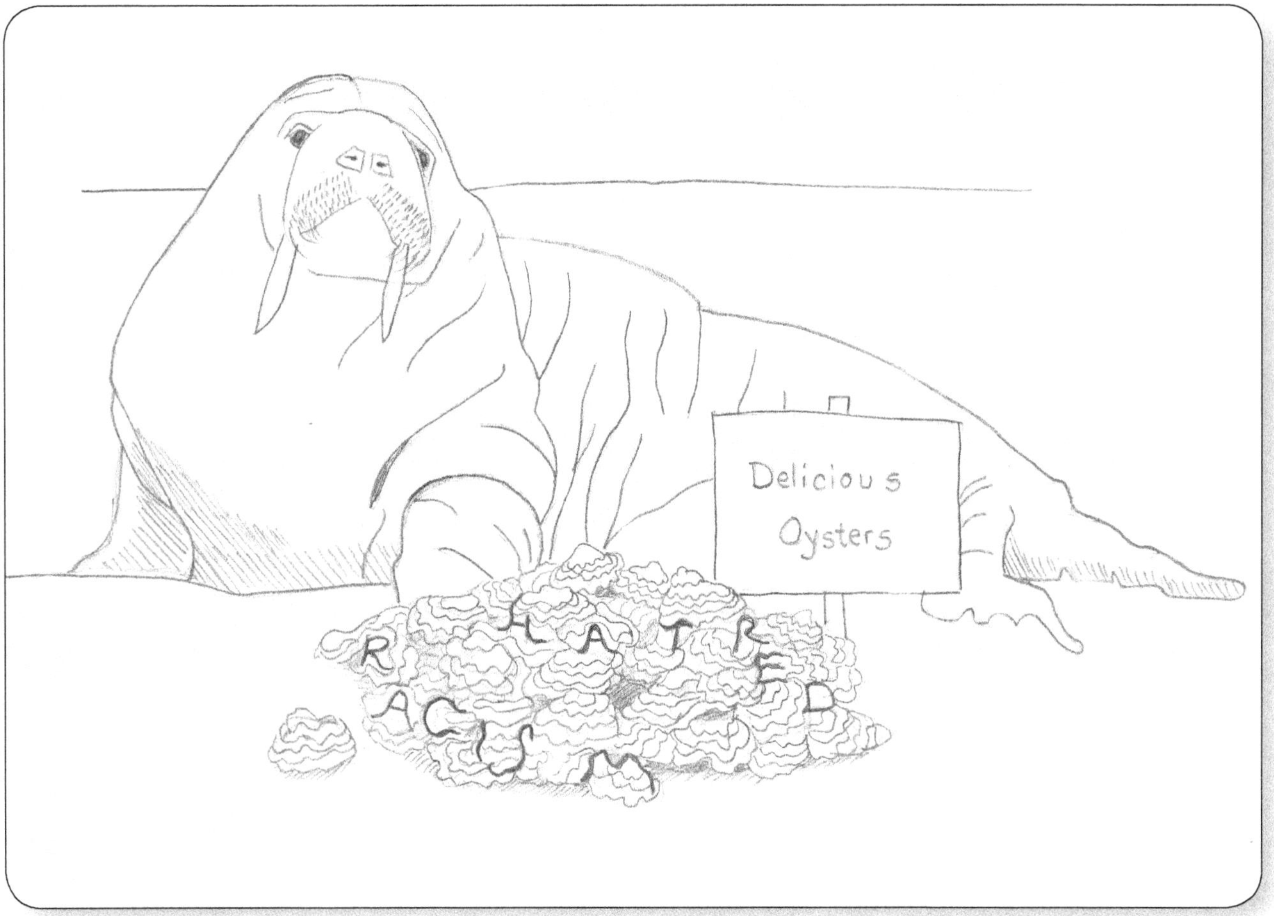
Delicious
Oysters

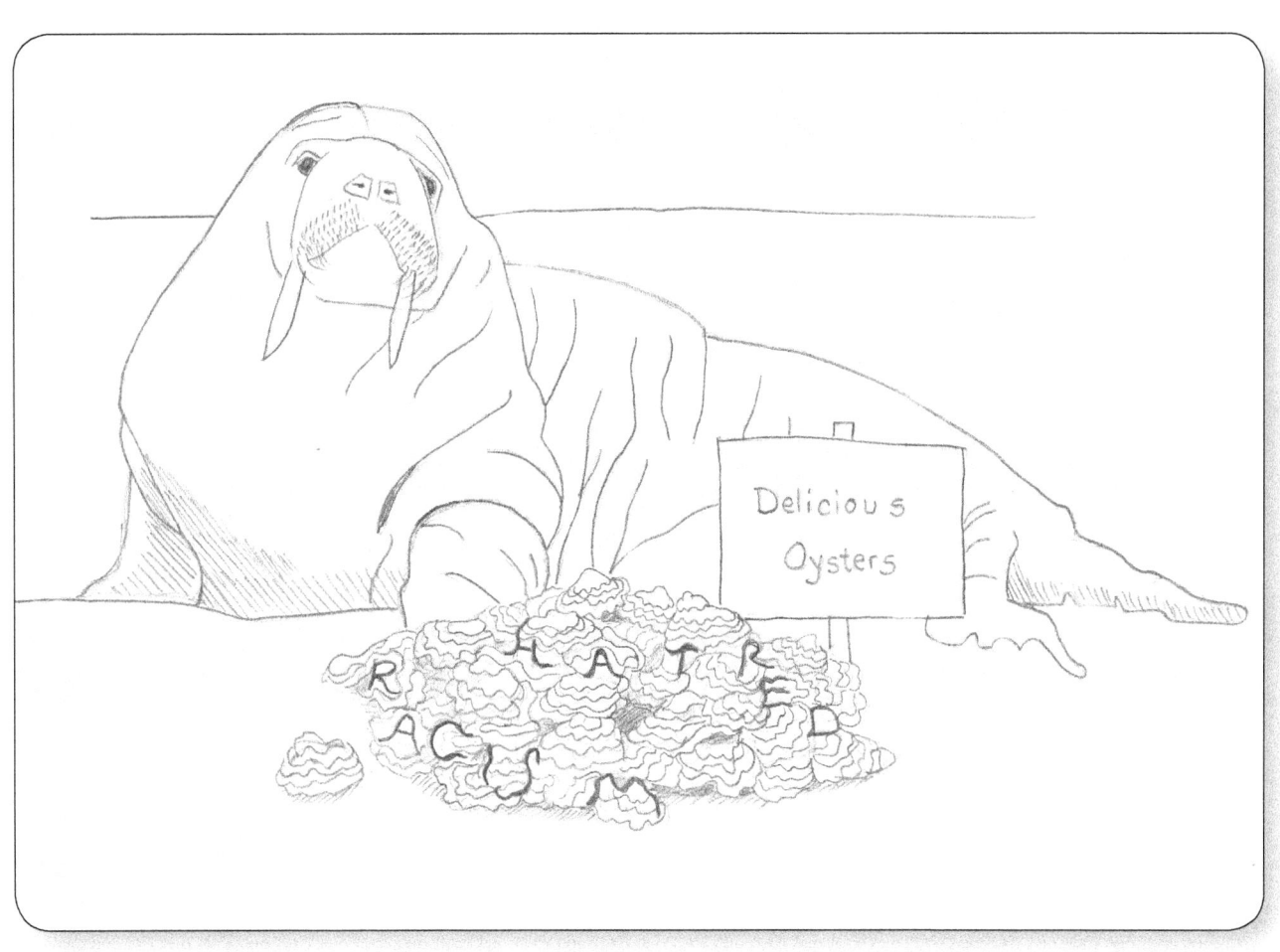

"I won, I won!" cried the mummer.
"I always knew that I could beat her.
Now the world can clearly see
That all the dogs love me, me, me!"

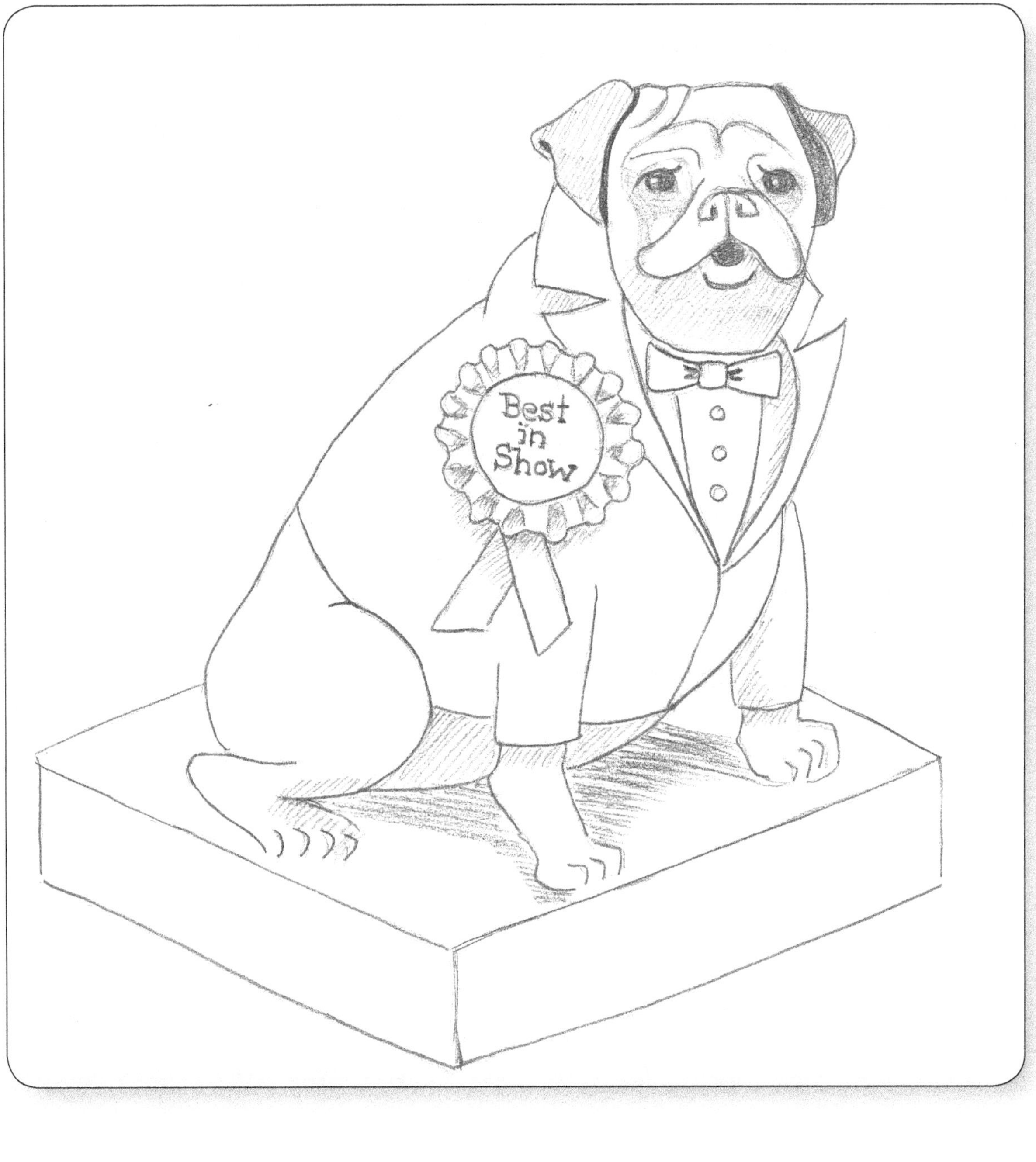
Best
in
Show

He climbed the platform high and proud

And heard the echo of the crowd.

Then the audience grew quite still

As a pup gave him a daffodil.

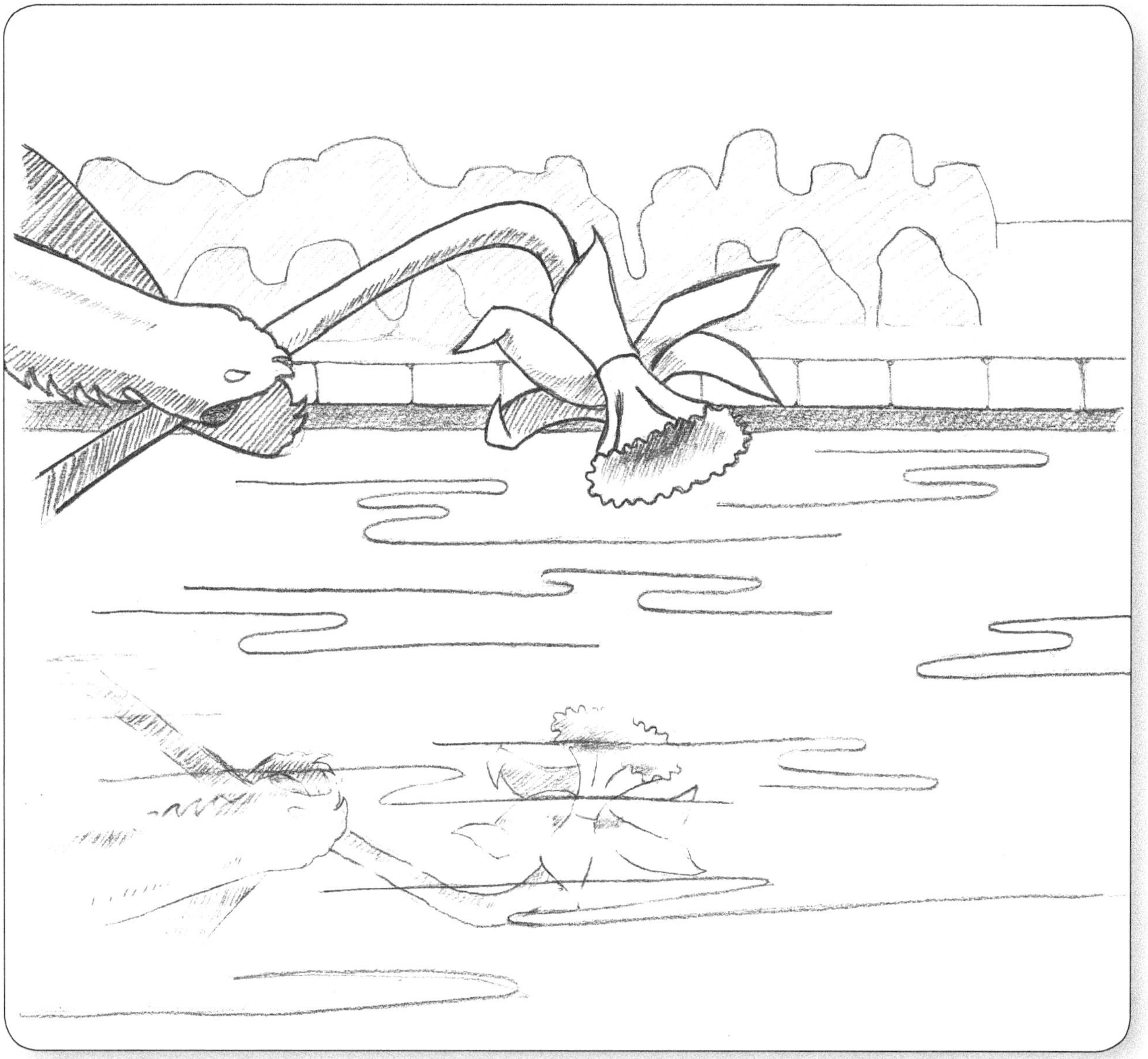

"I'll guard this flower like a jewel,"
He said while gazing at the pool.
And all his followers gathered 'round
To see their hero on the mound.

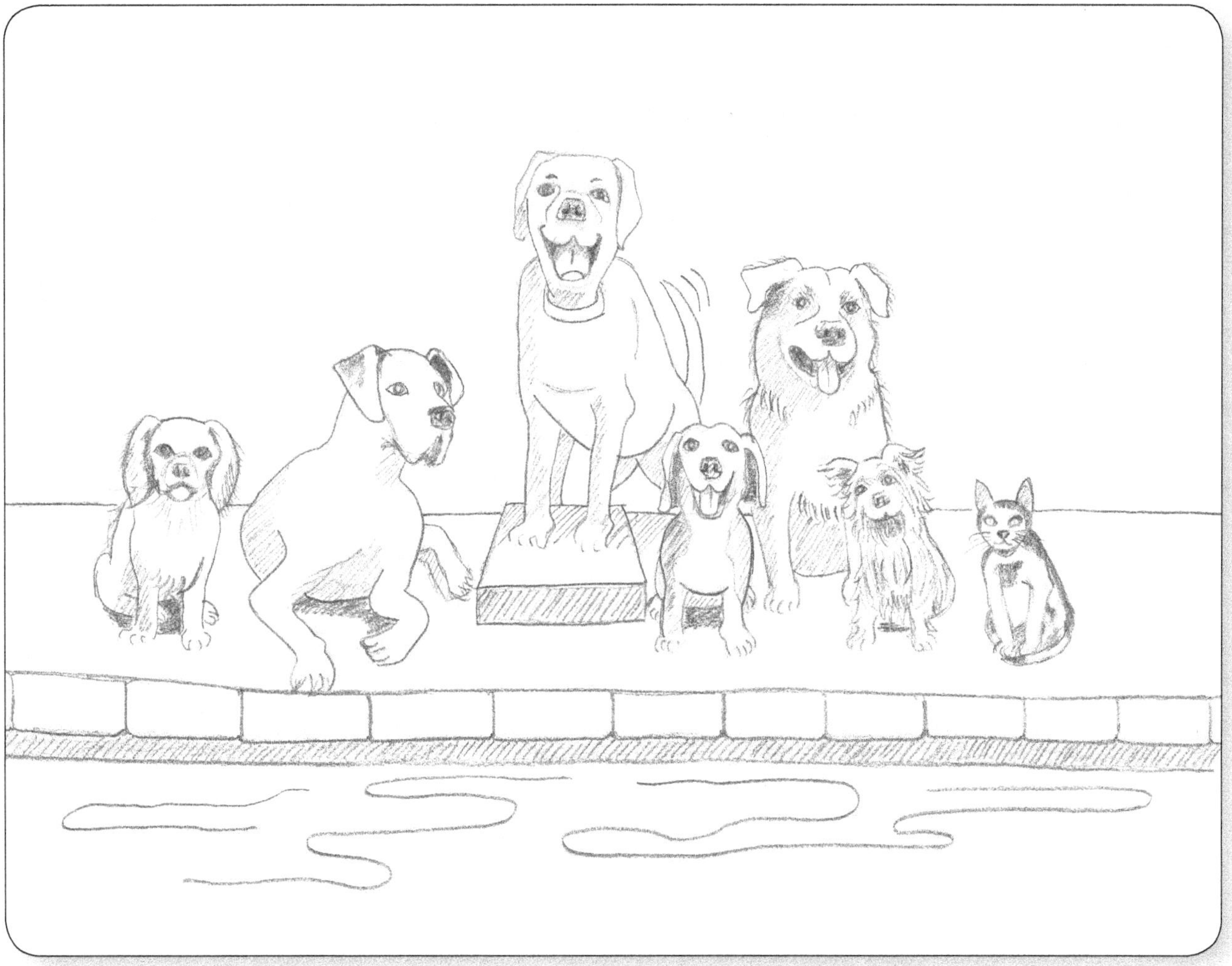

"But what was this uproar, this searing cry
And the press who says I lie, lie, lie?
The voters believe in me and my truth,
They showed this at the voting booth."

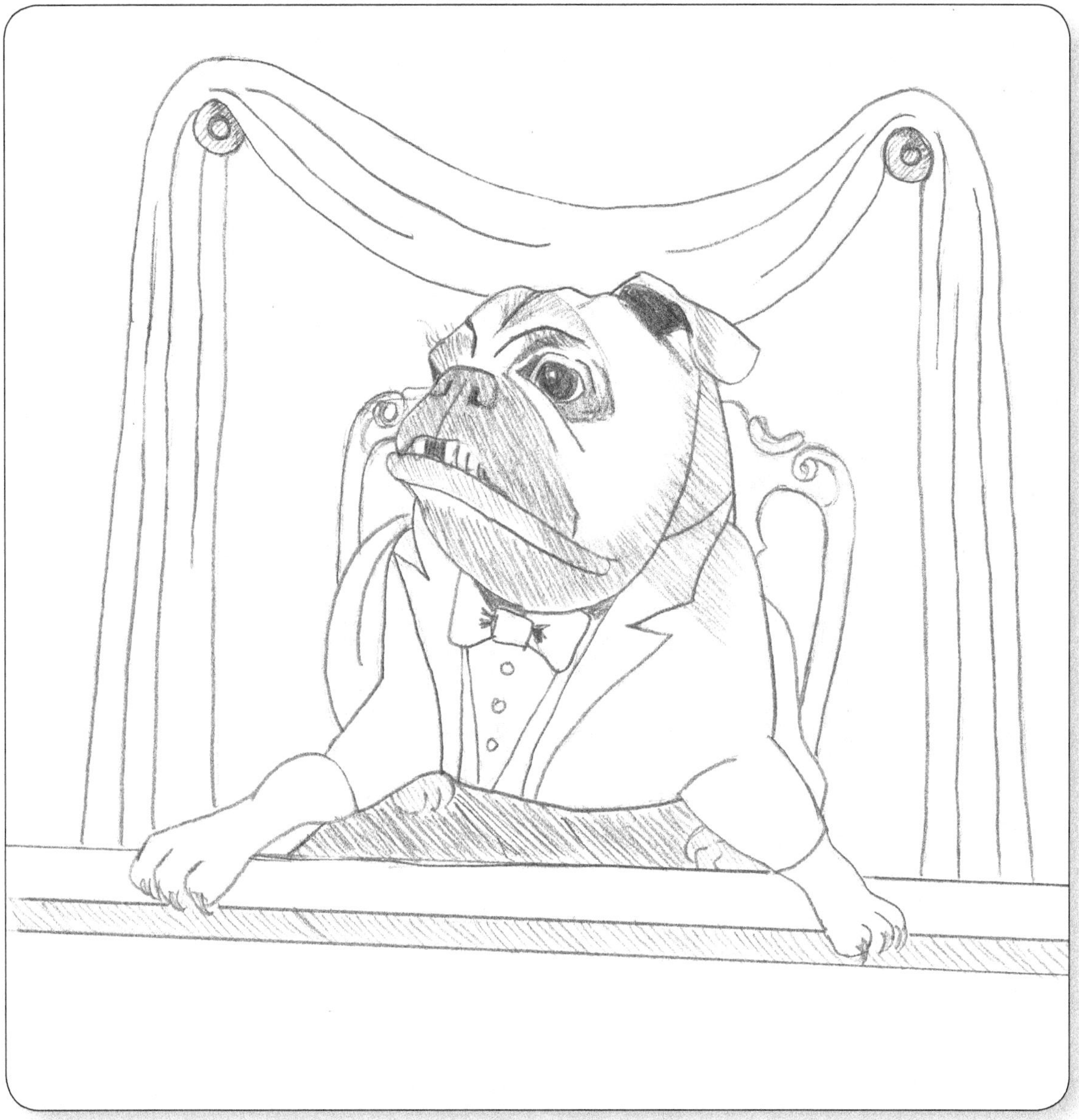

"Fake news should be a crime," he said,
"And I will judge what should be read.
Only approved stories will be run.
Arrest the reporters, every one."

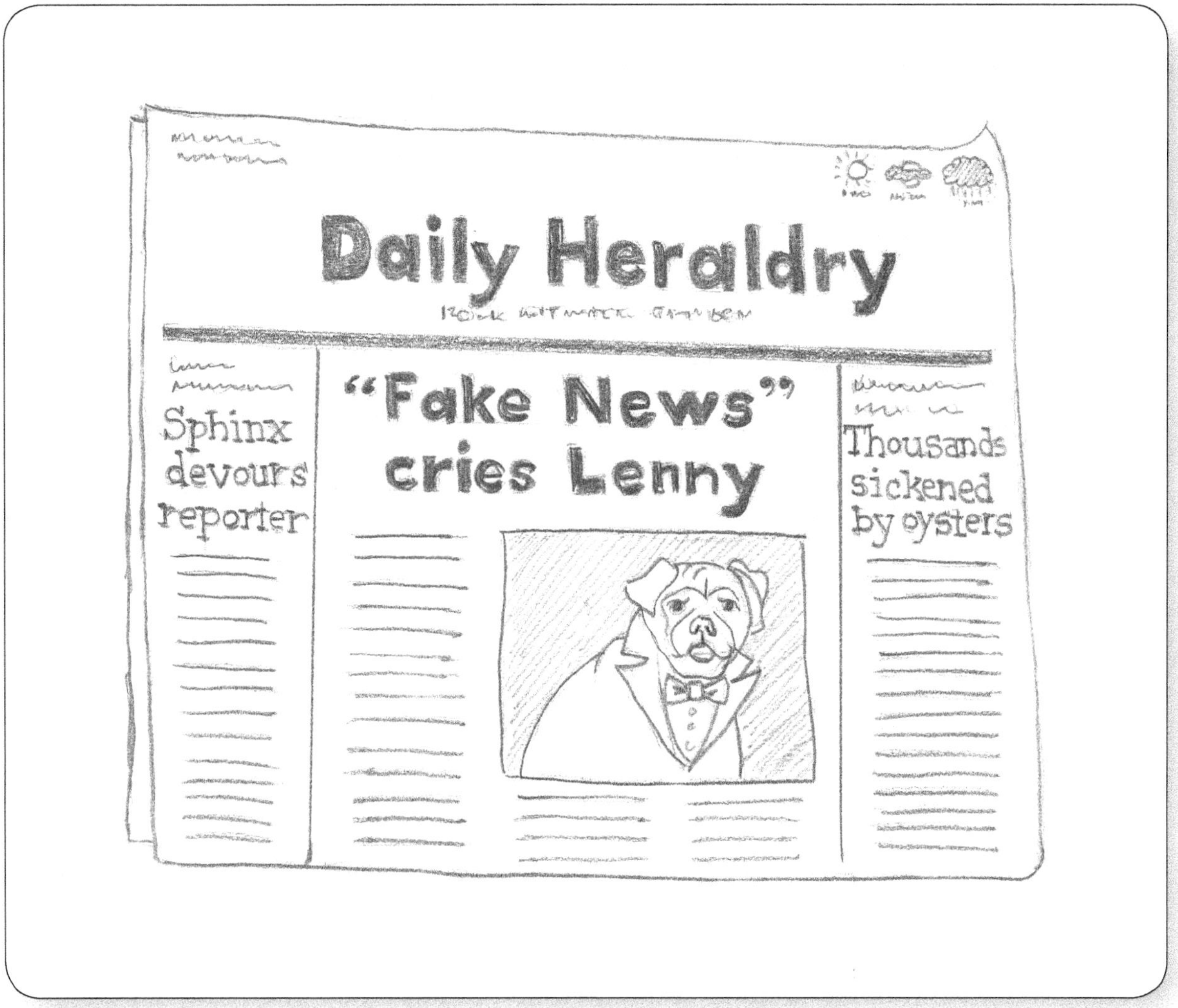

Daily Heraldry
"Fake News" cries Lenny
Sphinx devours reporter
Thousands sickened by oysters

And Lenny rose with a horrible growl,
With pursed lips and furrowed brow.
"I am king of the show," he said.
Then he shouted, "Off with their heads!"

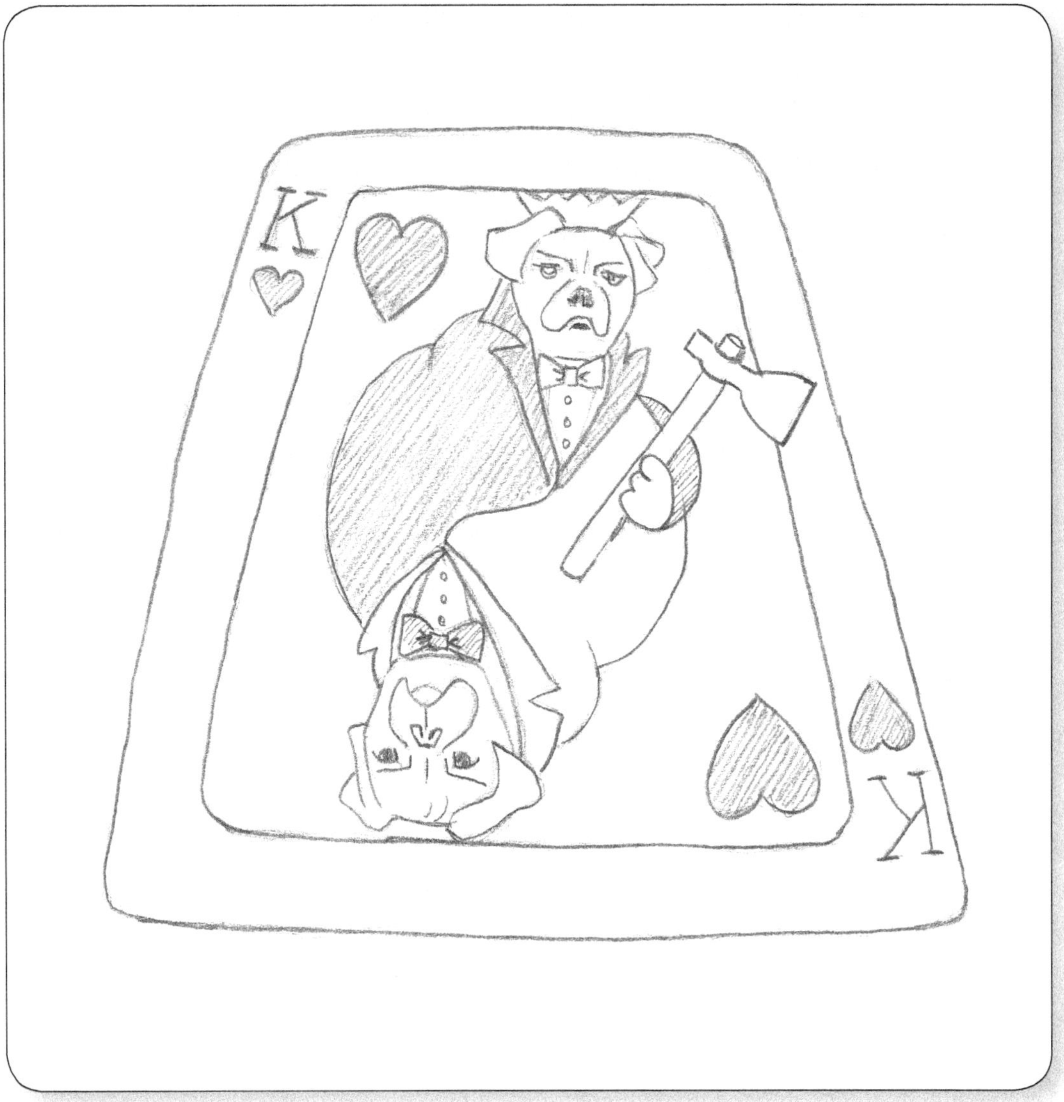
K
K

Lenny and the Very Big Show

Lenny of the golden tower
Had the money, wanted power
So he channeled P.T. Barnum
Just to see if he could charm 'em.

So like fish to bait are drawn,
Lenny's audience trailed along
To view the wonders of his show
And to see how far he'd go.

Others tried to face him down
But it was hard to best a clown.
He made crowds laugh, he made them roar
And then he showed his foes the door.

Now the bankers couldn't wait
To get part of the power and the gate.
They threw their money on the floor,
"Use our acts; we'll give you more."

So he hired the Sphinx to guard the gate
To riddle the press and make them wait.
He also brought the walrus along
To feed bay oysters to the throng.

Then Lenny brought his cast and crew
To the show to determine who
Through votes would win the golden ring
And be anointed queen or king.

"I won, I won!" cried the mummer.
"I always knew that I could beat her.
Now the world can clearly see
That all the dogs love me, me, me!"

He climbed the platform high and proud
And heard the echo of the crowd.
Then the audience grew quite still
As a pup gave him a daffodil.

"I'll guard this flower like a jewel,"
He said while gazing at the pool;
And all his followers gathered 'round
To see their hero on the mound.

"But what was this uproar, this searing cry
And the press who say I lie, lie, lie?
The voters believe in me and my truth.
They showed this at the voting booth."

"Fake news should be a crime," he said,
"And I will judge what should be read.
Only approved stories will be run.
Arrest the reporters, every one."

And Lenny rose with a horrible growl
With pursed lips and furrowed brow,
"I am king of the show," he said.
Then he shouted, "Off with their heads!"

— P.V. Larssen

AUTHOR'S NOTE

Lenny and the Very Big Show was inspired by childrens' nursery rhymes. As an adult I discovered that many of those rhymes had hidden meanings, often political. When I wrote this verse, I found myself referring back to books I have read and enjoyed over the years. Lewis Carroll's tales, *Alice's Adventures in Wonderland* and *Through the Looking-Glass* were both great sources of inspiration.

For many years I owned and enjoyed a book on Greek mythology, and was fascinated by the tales of warriors, heroes and tragedies. In my verse, I refer to tales of Echo and Narcissus, Hero and Leander and Oedipus encountering the Sphinx.

Something new I learned was the story of Jumbo, the circus elephant P.T. Barnum purchased from the London Zoo and brought to America to be a main attraction in his own very big show. That story was also a tragedy.

— P.V. Larssen

ACKNOWLEDGEMENTS

Thank you to my family for giving me support and encouragement during the creation of *Lenny and the Very Big Show*. They put up with my preoccupation and the mess of papers and drawings strewn all over the house.

Thanks also to my editors and pre-press friends, without whose help this would never have become a book.

Copyright © 2017 P.V. Larssen
All rights reserved
ISBN: 978-0-692-86902-4

This book contains images and text protected under International and Federal Copyright Laws and Treaties. No part of this book may be reproduced or transmitted in any form or by any means, electronic or mechanical, including photocopying, recording, or by any information storage and retrieval system without express written permission from the author.

Printed in the United States of America on paper that meets the
Sustainable Forestry Initiative Chain-of-Custody Standards.
WWW.SFIPROGRAM.ORG

www.ingramcontent.com/pod-product-compliance
Lightning Source LLC
Chambersburg PA
CBHW082248300426
44110CB00039B/2483